Parables for Christmas

Parables for CHRISTMAS

John Killinger

ILLUSTRATIONS BY
Florence S. Davis

ABINGDON PRESS
NASHVILLE

PARABLES FOR CHRISTMAS

Copyright © 1985 by Abingdon Press

Fifth Printing 1988

This book is printed on acid-free paper.

Library of Congress Cataloging in Publication Data

Killinger, John.
    Parables for Christmas.
      I. Christmas—Meditations. 2. Jesus Christ—Para-
bles.
      I. Title.
BV45.K53   1985   242'.33   85-9032

ISBN 0-687-30061-4

MANUFACTURED BY THE PARTHENON PRESS AT
NASHVILLE, TENNESSEE, UNITED STATES OF AMERICA

For Krister,
whose unfailing excitement
at Christmas
always rekindles
my own

Contents

Introduction

Christmas is always a time for stories—
stories about Mary, stories about shepherds,
stories about wise men, stories about Jesus.
Oddly enough, we seldom hear at
Christmastime the stories Jesus himself told—the
timeless, piquant, sometimes caustic and
searing, often beautiful and fetching stories
about life and the kingdom of God.

Parables for Christmas is aimed at overcoming
this deficiency. It is a collection of the stories of
Jesus retold in the language of Christmas, so
that ministers and teachers and parents will not
hesitate to read them to their various audiences
at Christmastime.

It is even possible that some of the stories,
told and retold for so long in their original
wordings, can now be heard in new ways because of the changes in language and imagery.

Every attempt has been made to preserve the
meaning and force of the parables as Jesus told

them. The theological center of each story—what renowned biblical scholar Joachim Jeremias calls the "single point" it wants to make—is still located precisely where the Master intended it. Only the language is different.

The parables are, as Denis de Rougemont once put it, "calculated traps for meditation." They lure us inside by their simple but deceptive narrative form. But once inside, we cannot get out again. We are caught forever in a new way of seeing ourselves and the world around us.

That is what Jesus wanted—for us to see everything from a new perspective. And that is what *Parables for Christmas* is intended to do, to help us *re-see* some things we may have been missing.

What better time to do it than at Christmas, when we celebrate the birth of the One who first told the stories?

JOHN KILLINGER

The Man Who Fell Among Muggers

LUKE 10:30-36

*A*nd Jesus said a certain man, while doing his Christmas shopping, fell among muggers, who stripped him of everything, beat him to within an inch of his life, and left him in an alley behind St. Luke's Church.

The minister came along on his way to a service, and, when he saw the man, hurried into the church, afraid of becoming involved. And likewise an elder of the church came by and hurried past, as frightened as the minister. He even dropped the holly wreath he was carrying and didn't return to pick it up.

But the neighborhood agnostic, who didn't even believe in exchanging Christmas presents, when he heard the poor man groaning, investigated and felt sorry for him.

Bringing his car around, he helped the man into it, ignored the blood on his velvet-pile seats, and drove him to City Hospital.

"Here," he said to the receptionist, who

presented him with a battery of forms. "This is my credit card, and he is my brother. Give him a private room and the very best of care, and, if it exceeds the limit of my charge account, I'll borrow the money and pay you. What the heck, it's Christmas Eve!"

Which of these three men, do you think, was neighbor to the man who was mugged? And which one had a merry, merry Christmas?

"He is my brother."

The Christmas Feast

MATTHEW 22:2-10; LUKE 14:16-24

The kingdom of heaven is like a certain mayor who decided to have a Christmas sing and big dinner in the town hall for all his friends. He sent out invitations marked R.S.V.P., but no one responded.

So he had his wife call them on the telephone and say that he had ordered six hams, a leg of beef, and fifty pounds of plum pudding.

But most of them made excuses, and a few were even abusive to her.

When the mayor heard this, he was extremely angry. "It will be a cold day in July when I ask them again!" he declared. "Wait till they want any favors from me!"

And he sent his sheriff over to the jail and had all the prisoners brought into the town hall, and they had the finest Christmas sing and the biggest feast most of them had ever imagined.

The
Coloring
in the Dough

MATTHEW 13:33; LUKE 13:20-21

*T*he kingdom of heaven is like food coloring, a few drops of which a mother took and put in her cookie dough, so that it colored all the Christmas cookies.

The Hired
Santa Clauses

MATTHEW 20:1-16

*I*t was the beginning of the Christmas shopping season, and the manager of a certain department store hired Santa Clauses to stand outside the store. A few days later, business was so brisk that he hired others to stand there too. A week before Christmas, buying was at an all-time peak, and the manager engaged still more Santa Clauses, so that his store was veritably surrounded by men in red suits ringing bells and wishing people "Merry Christmas."

On Christmas Eve, the manager called in all the Santa Clauses and gave them their pay envelopes. When they opened them, they discovered that they had all received the same amount.

"Hey!" demanded the ones who were hired first. "What is going on here? We have been pounding the pavement outside this store since Thanksgiving. We should have had a lot more than these other men."

The second group agreed. "And we should have had more than these last bums!" they said. "We have frozen our cans off a week longer than they did. It isn't fair to give us all the same pay."

"Why not?" said the manager. "Haven't I paid you what we agreed to? And besides, isn't this what Christmas is all about, that we are dealt with not according to our merit, but according to grace? So don't let it spoil your Christmas. Rejoice in the gift of a Savior!"

"We should have had more than these last bums!"

The Deacon
and the Wino

LUKE 18:10-14

*T*wo men entered the church on Christmas Day to pray. One was a deacon, dressed in a pinstripe suit and feeling very full of himself; the other was a wino who wandered in off the street to escape the cold.

The first stood among the poinsettias and prayed thus with himself: "God, I thank you that I am not as most people are, boorish, undisciplined, and stinking of booze, even as this wino is. I pay my church pledge and read my Bible every day."

And the wino, standing before the crèche with his cap in his hand, twisted it nervously and looked at the floor, saying, "God, have mercy on me, a sinner."

I tell you, this man left the church with a Christmas blessing, rather than the other, for he understood the true meaning of the Incarnation, that Christ came into the world to save sinners, not the self-righteous.

The True Packages and the False Packages

MATTHEW 13:24-30

*T*he kingdom of heaven is like a sixth-grade classroom in which all the students wrapped presents for one another and placed them under a Christmas tree. But when they had all been put there, some scoundrels got the bright idea of wrapping empty boxes and scattering them among the presents.

The students were unhappy with this, for they could not tell which presents were genuine and which were not. So they came to the teacher and asked, "Teacher, should we open all the presents now, and then rewrap the true ones?"

But she said, "No, for that will destroy the element of surprise when we open the real packages. Let the two sets of packages remain as they are until we have our party. Then we shall open all of them and burn the false packages."

The Christmas Account

MARK 4:26-29

So is the kingdom of God, as if a person started a Christmas savings account, and every week, as she was putting a few dollars into it, it was quietly and surely growing, almost without her consciousness of it. For the account was set to mature at the beginning of December. And when the time came, she went to the bank and drew it out full-grown and ready to spend.

The
Owner of the
Christmas Tree Farm

MARK 12:1-11; MATTHEW 21:33-44; LUKE 20:9-18

A certain man bought a large acreage in the north woods and started a Christmas tree farm there. Then he went away to a distant city where he had other business interests, and left the farm in charge of a local lumberjack.

As the years went by and he was receiving no income from the tree harvest, the man sent one of his accountants to look into things.

The accountant was roughed up by the lumberjack and some of his friends, and told never to show his face in those parts again.

The owner sent another employee, and he received the same treatment.

The next time, he sent two employees together, but they were beaten up so badly that one had to be hospitalized for three weeks.

At last the owner sent his son up to deal with the roughnecks, figuring that they would have respect for him, as he was the legal heir to the place. When they learned who he was, however, they said, "If we get rid of him, and the old man dies, we can keep this property for ourselves."

So they foully murdered the son and hid his body in a ditch on the tree farm.

How will the owner feel when he learns about this? Will he send the men a bonus and tell them they have done well?

He will not! He will stop at nothing until those evil men are destroyed and the tree farm is given over to persons who will acknowledge his ownership and faithfully send the proceeds to him.

"If we get rid of him, . . . we can keep this property for ourselves."

The
Ornament
of Great Price

MATTHEW 13:45-46

*A*gain, the kingdom of heaven is like a merchant who dealt in extremely valuable old Christmas ornaments and, when he found one made entirely of pearls and diamonds, he was so entranced by it that he sold his entire stock in order to buy that single ornament.

The
Christmas
Allowances

MATTHEW 25:14-30

A certain couple drove to the big city with their three children to shop for Christmas presents. After they parked the car, and the father had a conniption fit over the size of the parking fee, he and his wife gave each of the children money and instructions to find presents for other members of the family. To one child they gave fifty dollars, to another twenty, and to another ten.

"We'll meet back here at the car at five," said the father.

Now the child who had received fifty dollars rushed off to a large department store and immediately began to discover bargains.

Likewise, the one who had received twenty dollars hurried to a little boutique she had heard about and found some outstanding buys.

But the child who received ten dollars got sweaty palms, thinking, "Oh my, whatever shall I do with this ten dollars? If I am not careful, someone will pick my pocket, or I will go into a store and see something silly and make my folks mad by buying something they wouldn't like."

So this child took off his glove, poked the ten-dollar bill down into one finger, put the glove on, and spent the whole day standing in one spot, waiting for five o'clock to come.

At five o'clock, the family gathered again at the car.

"Let us see what you bought," said the parents.

"I'm dying to show you," said the child who had received fifty dollars. "I got such tremendous bargains. Why, this bed jacket for Aunt Lil is worth every penny you gave me, and it's only a small part of what I bought."

"Well-done," said the father, beaming with pride. "You've saved us so much money that I'm going to buy you a special dinner tonight!"

The second child—the one who received twenty dollars—was likewise excited to reveal what she had purchased.

"I found this fabulous record set for Ronnie," she said. "It had been marked down to half-price because of a smudge on the dust jacket. And look what else I found, too!"

Her parents beamed.

"Splendid!" said her father. "It looks as if we'll make that a special dinner for you, too. I have such wonderful children!"

Then he asked to see what the third child had

bought. The child seemed nervous and was struggling for something in his glove.

"Here, Dad," he said. "Here's your ten dollars back. I was afraid something would happen to it or that I would spend it foolishly, so I hid it in my glove. See? It's all there. I didn't even get change for it."

"You worthless child!" exploded the father. "You knew I brought you into the city to shop. And here I was, paying six dollars for a place to park the car, while you dawdled around all day with my money in your glove!"

Snatching the ten dollars from the child's hand, he put it in his billfold and took out two fives.

"Here," he said, giving one to each of the other children. "You deserve this. You can spend it on yourselves after we've had dinner. But as for you, young man, you can just sit here in the car until we come back. You don't deserve a good dinner."

And there was weeping and sadness in the car as the others went off arm in arm to find a good restaurant.

New Cloth
and Old

MATTHEW 9:16-17; MARK 2:21-22

LUKE 5:36-38

Nobody patches an old Christmas stocking
with a piece of new cloth, for it doesn't
look right. Neither does anyone wrap new
fruitcake in old cheesecloth, lest the cloth
crumble and be destroyed. But new fruitcake
must be wrapped in new cloth, so that both will
be properly preserved.

The Smart Cook

LUKE 16:1-9

There was a certain rich woman who discovered, shortly before Christmas, that her
cook was carrying off food from the kitchen.

And she called the cook in and said to her,
"After the party next week, I shall not require
your services any longer."

The cook was distressed, and thought,
"Whatever shall I do? I cannot find another job
like this one, and I am getting too old to do
institutional cooking. I am ashamed to go on
unemployment. I know—I will make friends with
those who can take care of me when I leave."

So, on an afternoon when she knew her
mistress would be out, she threw a lavish party
in the mistress's house, to which she invited
many of the mistress's friends. She prepared the
best foods from the pantry and served in elegant
style. The guests were so impressed that they
began to ask her if she would not come and
work for them.

When the mistress heard what had happened and how everyone was so impressed with her cook, she complimented the cook and said she could stay on indefinitely, for as many Christmases as she would. For people who have to get along in the world are often more resourceful than those sheltered in religious faith.

And I say to you, make all the friends you can through the opportunities of the Christmas season, that when you are unable to have Christmas any longer, they will remember you forever.

"I will make friends with those who can take care of me when I leave."

Can the Smashed Lead the Smashed?

MATTHEW 15:14; LUKE 6:39

*A*nd he spoke a parable to them: Can a man who has had too much eggnog lead another who has had too much eggnog? Won't they both drive into the ditch?

The Fir Tree Seed

MATTHEW 13:31-32;

MARK 4:30-32

The kingdom of heaven is like the tiny seed of a fir tree, which a bird carried and dropped in a fence row. It is one of the least of all seeds. But when it is grown, it will bear many strings of lights and countless decorations, and then tower over a multitude of gaily wrapped presents!

The
Christmas
Carolers

MATTHEW 13:3-9, 19-23;

MARK 4:3-8, 14-20; LUKE 8:5-8, 11-15

A group of carolers went forth to carol. And, as they caroled, some carols were lost on the evening air and simply disappeared in the night. And some fell on stony ears, and as soon as they were heard, they were forgotten. And some were caught up in the general noise of the street, which at times rose up and overpowered them. And other carols went straight to their mark and gladdened the hearts of those who heard them, so that they were hummed and repeated hundreds of times as these persons went about during the Christmas season. Whoever can understand this should give thanks for carols!

The Corporate Fool

LUKE 12:16-21

*A*nd he spoke a parable to them, saying that
the stocks and bonds of a certain rich man
took a sudden upward turn the week before
Christmas.

And the rich man thought within himself,
saying, "What shall I do? I could share the
benefits of this bonanza with my children and
grandchildren, but they would only squander
what I gave them. I could give a large donation
to the university, or to my church, but I don't
approve of the way they spend their money
these days. I think I shall erect a new
condominium and live well from the income for
the rest of my life. I can spend Christmas in
Acapulco and summers in Lucerne."

But God said unto him, "You fool, this night
your soul shall be required of you. Then who
will spend Christmas in Acapulco and summers
in Lucerne?"

So is he who lays up good things for himself
without considering God.

The Two Parties

LUKE 16:13

No person can enjoy two Christmas parties on the same evening—for either she will hate one and love the other, or will wish to stay at one and find the other tacky. Similarly, you cannot love both God and money.

The
Rich Man
and Cratchit

LUKE 16:19-34

*T*here was a certain wealthy Scrooge, who was clothed in silks and cashmeres and had country ham and oyster casserole whenever he wished them.

And there was a poor Bob Cratchit who lived in Scrooge's tenant house and was so undernourished he would have been glad for the bone of one of Scrooge's hams. And he was sick with cancer.

And it came to pass that Bob Cratchit died, and was carried by the angels to the heavenly Christmas party. Scrooge also died and was buried. And from the desert place where his spirit was soon scavenging for old tidbits of toast and grapefruit rinds, he looked up and saw Bob Cratchit at God's elbow, eating canapés and drinking from a silver punchbowl.

And he cried and said, "Oh, God, this is awful. Have mercy on me, and send Bob Cratchit over here with a ladle of that Christmas punch, for I am in terrible shape in this godforsaken place."

But God replied, "I'm sorry, Scrooge, but you had your chance. Remember, in your lifetime you received good things and Cratchit received bad things. But now the tables are turned. And, besides, there is a great gulf between that wilderness and this party, and it isn't easy for anyone to pass between the two."

Then Scrooge said, "I pray you, therefore, God, that you send old Cratchit to my father's house, where my five brothers are enjoying lobster thermidor and brandied pudding this Christmas Eve, that he may warn them lest they follow me to this godforsaken place."

God replied: "They have had plenty of preachers. Let that be enough."

"Oh, no," said Scrooge. "It will take more than that. I know. I was a faithful churchgoer myself. But if they were to behold someone from the dead—you know, a kind of ghost of Christmas Present, or something like that, they would pay attention."

"Sorry," said God. "If they haven't listened to their preachers, they won't listen to a ghost either. That's the way it is."

". . . that he may warn them lest they follow me to this godforsaken place."

*T*he Lost Child

LUKE 15:3-7

What person among you, taking one hundred children to the theater for a performance of *A Christmas Carol*, if you lose one of them, does not stand the other ninety and nine in the theater lobby and go in search of the one that is lost? And when you have found the little tyke, you take it in your arms with rejoicing.

And when you get back to the lobby, you say to the others, "Whee, everybody, I have found the lamb who was lost!"

I tell you, there is more hanging of evergreens in heaven over one sinner who repents than over ninety and nine just persons, who need no repentance.

The Lost Ornament

LUKE 15:8-10

What woman, having ten silver Christmas ornaments that have been in the family for years, and losing one of them, does not turn her house upside down to find it? And when she does find it, she calls in all her family and phones the neighbors, who were aware of her search, to say, "Come and have a cup of eggnog to share my joy with me. I have found the dear ornament that was lost!"

The Boy
Who Came Home
for Christmas

LUKE 15:11-32

A certain man had two sons. The younger one
said to his father, "Give me my Christmas
presents early this year. I am bored with this
place and am splitting for the big city."

And the father took the presents out of the
closet and gave them to him.

And not many days after, the son packed his
bag and took a long trip to the city, where he
wasted all his money in an endless round of
Christmas parties. He even hocked his father's
presents, and soon he had spent all that, too.

The minute he had run out of funds, doors
were closed to him and the party spirit was
over. In desperation, he went out and attached
himself to the owner of a Jewish delicatessen,
who sent him into the kitchen to wash dishes.
He was so hungry that he sneaked scraps of
food off the plates he was cleaning. And no one
said as much as a kind word to him.

Finally, on the day before Christmas, he came
to his senses. "How often," he thought, "have I
seen my father set hired help down to a

steaming meal at my mother's table, and I am stuck here eating this garbage! I am going to hightail it out of here and return home as fast as I can, and I will say to my father, 'Dad, you were right, it's a tough world, and I didn't make it. You don't owe it to me at all, but I would like to come home and work for you as a hired hand, if you'll have me.' "

He turned in his apron, collected the few dollars that were coming to him, and went directly to the bus station. All the Christmas lights seemed to blink warmly, as if they approved what he was doing, and the Santas on the street corners blessed him on his way.

He rode all night, rehearsing his speech as he went. "Dad, you were right, it's a tough world. . . . Dad, you were right. . . ."

At dawn on Christmas day, the bus pulled up outside the bus stop in his little hometown, and he tumbled off, wrinkled, unshaven, and a little worried about how it would be.

"Son!" a voice called. And there was his father.

"But, Dad, how—how did you know?" he stammered.

"How did he know?" said the old station agent, taking the morning papers off the bus. "Why, he's come down here two, three times a day, every day since you've been gone."

"Dad," said the boy, "it's a tough world, and you were right. . . ."

"I know," said the father, putting an arm

around the boy's shoulders. "Come, let's go home."

At home, he called for his wife and anybody else who was in the house and said, "Look who's here! Look who's here!"

And he brought out presents and laid them before his son, including a beautiful new bathrobe, a pair of nice leather slippers, and a handsome, sparkling ring.

"Here," he said, putting the ring on his son's hand. "Go take a nice, warm bath, and put on this robe and these leather slippers, and come down and we'll have a wonderful visit.

"Get out that standing rib roast we have in the freezer," he said to his wife. "And turn on the tree lights! We're really going to have a celebration today!"

Meanwhile, the elder son came in from taking Christmas presents to the father's business customers, saw all the lights, and smelled the roast cooking in the oven.

"Hey, what's going on?" he said. "This place has been like a morgue, and suddenly it's Christmas and the Fourth of July rolled into one!"

"It's your brother," his mother said. "He's come home. He's upstairs bathing; he'll be down in a few minutes."

Boiling with anger, the elder son stomped out of the house, slamming the door, and began chopping wood to relieve his fury. Soon the father came out to see him.

"What's eating you, son?" he said.

"You know darned well what's eating me!" said the elder son. "It's this son of yours! He goes off to the city, taking every penny he can get out of you, and all his Christmas presents too. And then he comes back here stinking like a bum and you throw your arms around him as if nothing had happened! I don't understand you. I have never done anything like that. I'm always in by ten o'clock. I've been a model child all my life, and I can't remember when you've ever served up a standing rib roast in my honor, or even a T-bone steak. Yet this mountebank son of yours comes back after taking you to the cleaners and you treat him as if he were the Son of God himself. That's what's eating me!"

The father watched the elder son driving the battered old wedge through a tough green log.

"Son," he said, "you're hurting yourself this way. You have been a model son in every way. But I don't love you for what you do; I love you for who you are. And I love your brother the same way. He has had a terrible time, but now he's home. Come on in, and let's have the most wonderful Christmas we've ever had. Your brother was as good as dead to us, but has come back to life. He was lost, but is found."

And I would like to say that the father put his arm around the elder son's shoulders, and they smiled at each other and entered the house together for the grandest Christmas celebration they had ever known. But that would be unrealistic, wouldn't it? Stories don't always have such beautiful endings.

"Dad, it's a tough world."

The Costume Party

MATTHEW 22:11-14

A woman who was giving a great Christmas
ball walked through the crowd of happy
revelers until she came to a young man who
was not in costume.

"You knew this was a costume party," she
said. "What are you doing here like that?"

And looking around at all the Dickensian and
fairy-tale characters, the young man was
speechless.

"Show him to the door," the woman said to
the butler. "This is my party, and people will
come as I tell them to come."

And the young man was put out in the dark,
with weeping and protestations. For many are
invited, but not all are allowed to remain.

The Unforgiving Businessman

MATTHEW 18:23-35

Therefore is the kingdom of heaven likened unto a certain credit manager, who noted shortly before Christmas that one of his store's customers owed a staggeringly large sum, on which, despite monthly billings, he had not paid a penny for over a year. Knowing the customer personally, the credit manager walked over to the customer's business office in a nearby building and accosted him about the account.

"I have no recourse," said the credit manager, "but to give this bill to our collection agency. And, of course, you will have no more credit with our store."

"Oh, please," said the businessman. "Not at Christmastime. I have more than I can bear. If you give me a bad credit rating, I'm as good as dead in this town. Be patient, I implore you, and I will pay every dime I owe you."

The credit manager, being a soft touch, looked at the lights of the Christmas tree glowing in the outer office.

"All right," he said. "I guess Christmas is a time for generosity. I'll take you off report, and maybe you can work out something after the start of the year."

But the customer went out that afternoon and found someone who owed his own business a paltry sum and, taking him by the lapels, threatened him if he did not immediately fork over the sum in question.

"Please, sir," expostulated the man, "it is Christmas, and I have spent everything on presents for my wife and children. Give me a few days, and I will have the money for you."

But the businessman was unrelenting, and placed the debt in the hands of a collector.

Now the businessman's secretary, when she learned he had done this, remembered the conversation she had heard that morning between her boss and the credit manager, and she went and told the credit manager what had happened.

Calling the businessman on the telephone, the credit manager gave him a severe tongue-lashing for what he had done.

"Shouldn't you have had as much Christmas spirit with that man," he asked, "as I had with you? Inasmuch as you didn't, I am putting you on report the instant I hang up this phone."

So will the heavenly Father do also unto you, if you in your heart cannot feel the spirit of Christmas toward your brothers and sisters.

"Please, sir, it is Christmas, and I have spent everything on presents for my wife and children."

*T*he Ten
Sorority Girls

MATTHEW 25:1-13

*T*hen shall the kingdom of heaven be likened
unto ten sorority girls who were chosen to
participate in the Great Christmas Pageant,
singing carols and bearing lighted candles down
the aisles to herald the coming of Santa Claus,
played by Robert Redford.

And five of them were wise, and five were
foolish. Those who were foolish neglected to get
any candles, thinking they would be provided.
The wise ones were careful to get their own
candles, lest none be provided for them.

Mr. Redford's plane was late in arriving, and
all the girls went to sleep as they waited.

At midnight, a cry went up from the student
body. Mr. Redford was emerging from a
limousine, dressed in a Santa suit.

The girls all arose, patted their dresses,
checked their make-up, and got ready to
precede Mr. Redford down the aisle.

When the girls without candles learned that

none would be provided, they were in a panic, and begged the other girls to share theirs.

But the wise girls answered, "No, we can't; we've only enough for ourselves. Why don't you run over to the all-night market and buy some?"

And while they went to the market, the orchestra began to play and Mr. Redford motioned that he was ready to go on stage. And those who had candles enjoyed the biggest moment of their lives, caroling and walking ahead of Robert Redford.

Afterward, when the foolish girls returned and tried to get Mr. Redford's autograph, he said, "Do I know you?"

Watch therefore, for you know neither the day nor the hour when the Son of man comes.

"Do I know you?"

It's Not What You Say, It's What You Do That Counts

MATTHEW 21:28-31

A certain woman had two children. And she said to one the week after Christmas, "Son, we have got to take the tree down and put up all the decorations; I can't stand this mess any longer."

And he said, "Not me, Mom; let Sis do it." But afterwards he softened up and began to take down the tree.

And the mother came to the daughter and said the same thing.

The daughter said, "Sure, Mom, I'll do it in a minute."

But she didn't do it.

Which of the two, do you think, did the will of the mother?

The first?

You're right.

And you know something else? Hookers and pimps will go into the kingdom of God ahead of some preachers and deacons.